**Discovering
Cultures**

Brazil

Robert Reiser

BENCHMARK BOOKS

MARSHALL CAVENDISH
NEW YORK

With thanks to Robert N. Anderson, Ph.D., Associate Director, Institute of Latin American Studies, UNC Chapel Hill, for the careful review of this manuscript.

Benchmark Books
Marshall Cavendish
99 White Plains Road, Tarrytown, New York 10591-9001
Text copyright © 2003 by Marshall Cavendish Corporation
Map and illustrations copyright © 2003 by Marshall Cavendish Corporation
Map and illustrations by Salvatore Murdocca
Book design by Virginia Pope
All rights reserved. No part of this book may be reproduced in any form without written permission from the publisher.

Library of Congress Cataloging-in-Publication Data

Reiser, Robert.
Brazil / by Robert Reiser.
p. cm. — (Discovering cultures)
Includes bibliographical references and index.
Summary: An introduction to Brazil, highlighting the country's geography, people, foods, schools, recreation, celebrations, and language.
ISBN 0-7614-1180-1
1. Brazil—Juvenile literature. I. Title. II. Series.
F2508.5 .R45 2003
981—dc21   2001007292

Photo Research by Candlepants Incorporated
Cover Photo: Getty Creative/Stone/Will and Deni McIntyre

The photographs in this book are used by permission and through the courtesy of; Corbis: AFP, 1; Michael S. Lewis, 4-5; Owen Franken, 6, 20-21; Richard List, 8; Robert Homes, 9; Eye Ubiquitous, 10; Jan Butchofsky, 12; David Katzenstein, 13, 24; Jeremy Horner, 14-15; Wolfgang Kaehler, 16, 17, 18, 22, 26-27; Massimo Listri, 19; Stephanie Maze, 25, 36; Arvind Garg, 28, 33; Temp Sport, 30-31; Carl and Ann Purcell, 32; Reuters NewMedia Inc., 37, 40, 44; Inge Yspeert, 38-39. Getty Creative: The Image Bank/Anthony Boccaccio, 11; The Image Bank/ Andy Caulfield, 34; Stone/ David Frazier, back cover. Imperial Museum-IPHAN, Institute of the National Historical and Artistic Patrimony, 45.

Cover: *Offices and apartment buildings crowd the coast of Rio de Janeiro.*
Title page: *A musician wearing a golden costume participates in a Carnaval parade.*

Printed in Hong Kong

1 3 5 6 4 2

Turn the Pages...

Boa vinda ao Brasil!

(Welcome to Brazil!)

Two young Brazilians in a park

Where in the World Is Brazil?

Brazil is located south of the United States, just below the equator. It is the largest country in South America and home to 160 million people. Brazil is almost as big as the United States, but it looks very different on a map. The country is shaped like a giant face looking east toward the Atlantic Ocean.

Brazil has one of the longest coastlines in the world. It is made up of beautiful beaches and busy cities such as Rio de Janeiro. *Pampas* (prairies) and rolling hills cover the southern part of the country, where *gaúchos* (cowboys) and large herds of cattle roam. In the southeast, the Iguaçu River tumbles down the mountains into 275 waterfalls at Iguaçu Falls. Central and western Brazil is a high, cool plateau of mountains, grasslands, and swamps.

A rainbow arches over Iguaçu Falls.

Atlantic Ocean

Amazon River

Amazonia

Sertão

Brasília

Iguaçu Falls   Iguaçu River   São Paulo

Rio de Janeiro

N
NW   NE
W   E
SW   SE
S

Rain forests line the banks of the Amazon River.

To the north, the Amazon rain forest covers almost half the country. The Amazon River flows through the rain forest. It is the largest freshwater river in the world. The Amazon is so wide that it can take a day to sail across during the rainy season!

Some parts of Brazil are hot and wet. One such place is Amazônia, the deep green valley of the Amazon River. But in the Sertão, in northeastern Brazil, it is so dry that hardly anything can grow there. Farmers struggle with droughts that sometimes last for years. Other areas are temperate. The weather does not get

Coffee beans ripen in the sun.

too hot or too cold. Because Brazil is south of the Equator, its seasons are opposite those in the United States. Southern Brazil is cold enough to have snow in July but warm enough to go swimming in December.

Brazil's fertile soil produces a variety of crops. Twenty-five percent of the world's coffee grows on the plateau around São Paulo. Heavy rains help the sugarcane to grow along the east coast, making Brazil one of the world's largest sugar producers. Many of the country's other important resources, such as aluminum, zinc, tin, and gold, lie beneath the earth's surface.

Brasília is known for its modern architecture.

In the heart of Brazil stands the nation's capital, Brasília, one of the most modern cities in the world. The country's leading architects, Lúcio Costa and Oscar Niemeyer Soares, designed and built it in the 1960s. Two million people live in this fantastic city.

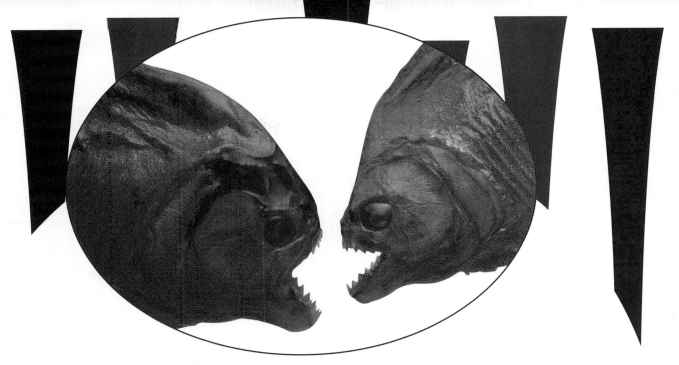

The Rain Forest

More than one million different kinds of plants and animals live in the rain forest of northern Brazil. Fig and banana trees are covered with fruit. Mushrooms pop up from the forest floor. Colorful parrots call down from the crowded canopy a hundred feet overhead. Monkeys swing through the trees. Capybaras swim in the rivers. These mammals are cousins of the guinea pig, but they can weigh up to 150 pounds (68 kilograms)! Capybaras are not the only strange swimmers. Piranhas are dangerous meat-eating fish with razor-sharp teeth. People are careful to avoid these fish when they go into the water.

The rain forest may seem unusual, but it has given us many familiar gifts. Imagine your car or bicycle without rubber tires. Today most tires are created from man-made rubber. However, at one time most of the world's natural rubber came from the rubber trees of the Amazon River basin. Do you like tapioca pudding? Tapioca comes from the Brazilian manioc tree, which grows in the rain forest. And millions of rain-forest trees produce oxygen for our planet. These are just some of the reasons that many people work hard every day to protect this amazing habitat.

What Makes Brazil Brazilian?

Like the United States, Brazil is home to people who come from other lands. Asians and Europeans live in the cool parts of the country. Hundreds of years ago, the Portuguese brought African slaves to Brazil. Their descendants still live there. Brazil has one of the largest populations of people of African descent outside of Africa today. Some of Brazil's native people, such as the Yanomami, have lived deep in the Amazon rain forest for thousands of years. Brazil is proud of its citizens, most of whom are a blend of these different cultures.

The ways Brazilians dress highlight their differences. If you look down a city street in Brazil, you will see children in jeans, T-shirts, and skirts, just like in the United States. Grown-ups wear sport

Brazilians come from many different backgrounds.

Gaúchos *herd cattle in the* pampas.

shirts, jackets, suits, and dresses. However, in the *pampas*, *gaúchos* wear wide-brimmed hats and wrap bandannas around their necks. And along the Amazon River, the Yanomami decorate themselves with beautiful red, white, and green paint and feathers.

What holds together such a large country with so many different people? The language is very important. Brazil was settled by Portugal five hundred years ago, so almost everyone in the country speaks Portuguese. Music is also important. Brazilians combined African, European, and native music to create entirely new rhythms, such as the *samba* and the *bossa nova*. Throughout Brazil, people rap out the *samba* on drums and other percussion instruments.

Family, friends, and conversation are at the heart of Brazilian culture. Any event —a wedding, a holiday, a birthday party, or a graduation—is an excuse to get together.

Food is also a big part of the culture. Do people drink coffee in your house? Almost everyone in Brazil does, even children. People drink it with milk and sugar, or they drink it black and strong, served in little cups.

Drummers beat Brazilian rhythms in the street.

15

Families enjoy being together.

Do you like family barbecues with hamburgers and hot dogs? Brazilian cook-outs are among the best. They call their barbecues *churrascos*. Every kind of meat that you can imagine is cooked over a wooden fire.

Brazil is a country for everyone. The government outlawed slavery in 1888, and discrimination against people because of race or religion is against the law. Even though racism still exists, Brazil wants to be a country where all citizens are treated equally.

Native People

The rain forest inspires the songs, dances, religions, and customs of the native people of the Amazon River basin. Native cultures respect both the gifts and the dangers of the jungle. People tend small gardens of fruits and vegetables, moving them after a few years to new clearings burned in the forest. This helps to refresh the soil. They climb tall trees to hunt monkeys and wade in the river to catch fish, such as the 60-pound (27-kilogram) tambaqui. But they never take more than they can eat. They know how to be keepers of the rain forest.

With the construction of factories and farms in the rain forest, many native people have lost their lands. Recently, the government of Brazil has recognized these people as national treasures in need of protection. They have given some groups, such as the Kayapó and Yanomami, their own land, where they can live undisturbed. Still, many of Brazil's native people are in danger, so the work to save them goes on.

Living in Brazil

Brazilian homes come in different shapes and sizes. Many people live in houses in large cities such as São Paulo or Rio de Janeiro. Some Brazilians live in apartments in modern glass buildings high above the streets of the capital city of Brasília. Others live in tiny two-room farmhouses in the country or in tin shacks in the *favelas* (slums). And even today, there are native peoples living in *malocas* (straw huts) deep in the rain forest.

The Amazon River flows past a small rain-forest hut.

A house in São Paulo

Brazilians usually begin the day with a small breakfast of fresh fruit, bread, and sweet coffee with milk. They eat their big meal in the early afternoon. That is when the family may get together to share *feijoada*. So many people love this stew of black beans, beef, sausage, pork, onions, and garlic that it is sometimes called Brazil's national dish. In the evening, the family gathers again for a light supper of salads and *salgadinhos*. These bite-size pies are filled with shrimp, chicken, pork, or vegetables. Brazilians rarely use their fingers when they eat. Even if they are eating a hamburger or sandwich, they will hold the food with a napkin.

The most important meal of the week comes on Sunday. That is when the whole family may get together for a *churrasco*. In Brazil, family means more than brothers, sisters, and parents. It means cousins, second cousins, grandparents,

Cookouts are popular at the beach.

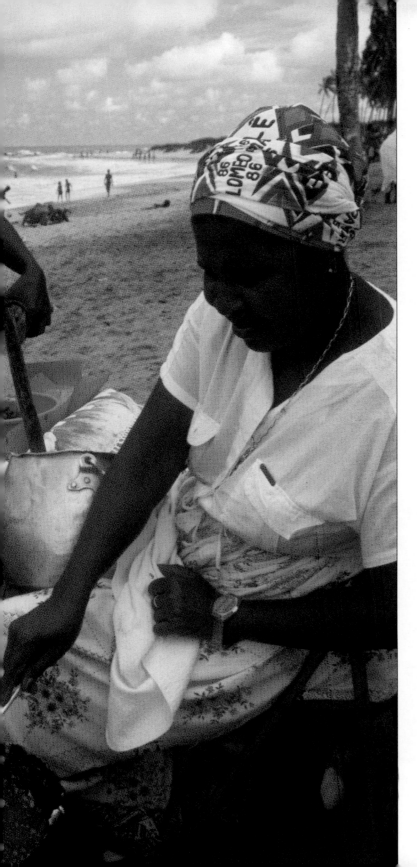

and even *padrinhos* (godfathers) and *madrinhas* (godmothers). After eating a big meal, as evening begins and the fireflies come out, the whole family stays to talk and drink *cafezinhos* (little cups of coffee). Brazilians love conversation, and they consider family to be a person's most valuable possession.

Going to the market is almost as much fun as a Sunday *churrasco*. In the cities, Brazilians shop at supermarkets just like the ones in the United States. The shelves are full of Brazil's favorite soft drinks made from fruits like *guaraná* and *goiaba* (guava). Popular cheeses like Queijo de Minas fill the dairy cooler. Put together a slice of *minas* cheese and some guava jelly for a delicious dessert called Romeu e Julieta. In another dairy cooler, you will find milk. But something might surprise you. The milk is not in bottles or cartons. It is in plastic bags!

Brazilians also shop in outdoor markets for fresh fruits unlike any in the world—tiny sweet bananas and

delicious oranges called *laranjas do céu* (heaven's oranges). They also buy papayas, pineapples, coconuts, and a root called *mandioca*. This white root is probably the most important food in Brazil. People eat *mandioca* raw, cooked, or dried into a tasty powder that can be sprinkled on dishes like *feijoada*. Food, family, and fun—these are the things that make life wonderful in Brazil!

A vendor sells pineapples at an outdoor market.

Let's Eat!
Brigadeiros

These favorite treats are named after a famous Brazilian Air Force commander, Brigadeiro (Brigadier General) Eduardo Gomes. Both children and adults love to eat them, especially at birthday parties. Ask an adult to help you prepare this recipe.

Ingredients:

1 can sweetened condensed milk

$1/2$ stick butter or margarine

2 tablespoons chocolate milk powder

Wash your hands. Mix chocolate powder and condensed milk in a heavy saucepan. Add butter or margarine. Cook on low heat, stirring until you can see the bottom of the pan. Continue stirring for two more minutes. Pour onto a plate and cool. Butter your hands and form the cooled mixture into little balls. Roll the balls in chocolate powder and serve them in small paper cups.

School Days

A student writes quietly at her desk.

In Brazil, the school year begins in March and ends in December. Summer vacation is in January and February. Why? Remember, Brazil's seasons are just the opposite of those in the United States.

Children who are seven to fourteen years old attend the *ensino fundamental* (elementary school). They walk or take a city bus, since school buses are uncommon in Brazil. Because the country has so many children and too few schools and teachers, students only spend half a day in school. They go in the morning from 7 A.M. to 12 P.M. or in the afternoon from 1 P.M. till 6 P.M.

When children get to school, they line up outside. In some

A Brazilian girl reads to the class.

schools, the boys and girls wear uniforms—white shirts with dark pants for boys and white shirts with dark skirts for girls. No jeans allowed! Nobody wears sneakers, except on the playground. In Brazil, school is a place for serious work and study, so children must dress appropriately.

In the classroom, students learn math, reading, writing, history, science, and language. Because many Brazilians come from different countries, children often

grow up speaking another language at home. In school, though, teachers make sure that every child can read and write Portuguese, the national language.

After about two and a half hours of studying, students go to the cafeteria for lunch. It is important for children to eat their school lunches. Some of them are so poor that this is the only nutritious meal they get all day.

When lunch is over, it is time for recess. Friends can climb the jungle gym or play ball or *pega-pega* (tag). Children in the older grades might play soccer, Brazil's favorite sport. After recess, it is back to the classroom for more reading and writing. Children also study music and learn traditional Brazilian songs. And they study the environment, identifying the plants and animals that live on their land.

Unfortunately, many poor children leave school before they are ten years

Children study the local animals, such as this sloth and this parrot.

old. They go to work to help their families. Schools try very hard to keep children from leaving. They allow working students to attend classes part-time. And at the age of eighteen, they offer every Brazilian who wants to go to college the chance to take a special exam called a *vestibular*. This test is very difficult, but if students pass, the government pays for their education. College students are very important to Brazil. They are the country's future doctors, lawyers, architects, and scientists.

Computer skills are important in a modern world.

Dominó Didático

Some Brazilian children practice their reading skills by playing a card game called Dominó Didático. There are twenty-eight cards in the deck. Each card has two different cartoons on one side, showing a pig, caterpillar, rabbit, dog, or dragonfly. The cartoons have a Portuguese word or phrase next to them. The cards are dealt to two to four players, who take turns placing the cards faceup with the cartoons showing. The object of the game is to match a cartoon on one card to a cartoon on another card, just like dominoes. The first player to match all his or her cards wins.

Just for Fun

School is out. Work is done. What do Brazilians do for fun? Many play soccer. The players seem to dance as they run down the field, kicking the ball from foot to foot, passing it to a teammate, and popping it into the air with their knees or foreheads. Called *futebol*, soccer is to Brazil what baseball is to the United States. Some of the greatest soccer players in the world are Brazilian. It is no wonder, since the country has more than 12,000 organized teams.

By the time he is five years old, almost every Brazilian boy knows how to play soccer. When he cannot play on a field, he plays on the beach, indoors, or in the street. He dreams of being the next great soccer star, like Pelé.

When Brazil plays in the World Cup soccer tournament, everything comes to a stop. Traffic disappears. Work ends. The streets become empty. Everyone listens to the radio or watches television to follow the game. When Brazil wins, fans in every

Fans cheer as a soccer player chases the ball.

Both the young and old enjoy a good soccer game.

city break out banners and dance down the streets wearing the green and yellow team colors. People light fireworks, sing, and dance the *samba* until dawn.

In addition to soccer, Brazilians love to play *capoeira*. This popular game combines dance, martial arts, and music. *Capoeira* began in Africa and was developed in Brazil by slaves and free people of African descent.

To play *capoeira*, a group of people make a circle called a *roda*. The music begins. One person plays a tambourine called a *pandeiro*, another plays a drum called an *atabaque*, and a third plays a stringed instrument called a *berimbau*. Everyone starts to clap. Two players step into the circle and face each other. They strut, they twirl, and they threaten each other with fancy headstands and somersaults, all in time to the music. No hitting is allowed. The idea is to get as close as you can to the other person without hurting him. This creates a beautiful dance that is sometimes called a fight with a smile.

Capoeira *dancers perform for a crowd.*

Brazilians enjoy watching TV as much as people in the United States. The most popular TV shows are *telenovelas* (soap operas). Every evening, adults turn on TV Globo to see the latest episode of their favorite *telenovela*. There are TV shows just for children, too. Xuxa (pronounced SHOO-shah) makes funny jokes as she invites children to play games and sing on TV.

Children also like to read the comics. One of the most popular follows the adventures of the lovable Monica and her friends in *Monica's Gang*. If children cannot wait for the next comic book to be published, they can read about her in the newspaper or on the Internet.

34

The Beach

Although Brazil has both very rich people and very poor, many of them love to go to the beach. Most Brazilians live no more than a short ride from the ocean. People who live farther inland often go there on vacation. Miles of beautiful white beaches attract artists, politicians, soccer players, laborers, and business executives. "Here there are no rich or poor," explained one Brazilian scientist. "In a bathing suit, everyone looks the same."

On the beach, people exercise, jog, make friends, and play volleyball and soccer. It is a busy, noisy place with vendors walking back and forth selling a kind of tea called *mate* or a soft drink known as *guaraná*. Children run up and down the sand flying kites or hitting a *peteca*, a sand-filled leather ball with feathers.

Let's Celebrate!

It is June 24. In São Paulo, a huge bonfire leaps seventy feet into the air. In Brasília, banners float against the sky and people wear silly tattered costumes like scarecrows. In Rio de Janeiro, fireworks burst all around. Across Brazil, candlelit paper balloons float in the night. Children sing as they watch the balloons catch fire and drop like falling stars. This is the feast of Saint John.

In Brazil, the month of June is one big party. It is the beginning of Brazil's festival season. The country celebrates the feast days of Saint Anthony, Saint John, and Saint Peter. In every town, streets turn into fairgrounds with tents, music and dancing, and games. People hold hands as they stroll through the streets munching on snacks such as sweet popcorn.

The festivals continue with the national celebration of Independence

Young girls display the flag on Independence Day.

Day on September 7. Brazil's southern states also celebrate another independence day, the Feast of the Cowboys. In 1835, the *gaúchos* rebelled against Brazil and tried to make their own country, called Rio Grande. After years of fighting, they decided to remain part of Brazil. Today, the *gaúchos* are still proud of their independent spirit. On September 20, they get together to honor the heroes of their past.

All day there are parades, songs, and rodeos with horseback riding and roping competitions. In the evening, the streets fill with dancers and children pretending to be *gaúchos*. People tell wonderful stories about Saci Pereré, an imaginary boy who lives on the *pampas* and plays tricks on cowboys.

A gaúcho *shows off his riding skills during a rodeo.*

In December, Brazilians celebrate Christmas. Even though it is summertime in their country, people decorate Christmas trees with silver icicles. Then children wait for Papai Noel (Santa Claus) to fill their shoes with gifts. On Christmas Eve, groups of traveling musicians called *reisados* go from house to house playing maracas, drums, flutes, and guitars. They perform special dances such as the Dança da Sorte (The Luck Dance) and Curiaba, which is about a little monkey.

The whole family gathers late at night for a big turkey dinner on Christmas Eve. This dinner would not be complete without *rabanadas*. Brazilians prepare a big batch of this favorite dessert to serve to visitors during the holiday week. *Rabanadas* are made like French toast. Pieces of French bread are dipped in milk and beaten eggs, then fried golden brown and sprinkled with cinnamon and sugar.

Holiday decorations light up the night.

Carnaval

The festival season closes with an event that Brazilians wait for all year—Carnaval! Celebrated at the end of February or in early March, four days before Ash Wednesday, Carnaval is a very old holiday. Originally, it was the last time that Catholics could eat meat before Lent. Today, Carnaval is a week-long party!

Every city in Brazil has its own celebration with parades, dances, and wild costumes. The biggest is in Rio de Janeiro. People wear brilliant colors and sing and dance the *samba*. They twirl red, yellow, and black umbrellas as they whirl down the street dressed in wild hats. The parade continues all day and night.

The celebration ends with Maracatu, the crowning of the king and queen of Carnaval. The most beautiful woman and the fattest man in the parade always win the crowns. Then everyone joins in one last dance that goes on until dawn. Festival season is over, but it will begin again in June.

The stars on the Brazilian flag represent the tropical sky, as well as the country's twenty-six states. The green stands for the thousands of plants that grow on the land, and the gold diamond represents the earth's buried treasures.

Brazilian currency, or money, is called the Real. The exchange rate often changes, but currently one American dollar equals 2.45 Reais.

Count in Portuguese

English	Portuguese	Say it like this:
one	um	OONG
two	dois	DOYS
three	três	TRAYS
four	quatro	KWAH-troo
five	cinco	SEEN-koo
six	seis	SAYS
seven	sete	SEHT-chee
eight	oito	OY-too
nine	nove	NAW-vee
ten	dez	DEHS

Glossary

capoeira (kah-pooh-AY-rah) Game that combines dance, martial arts, and music.

capybara (kap-ih-BAH-rah) World's largest rodent; looks like a large guinea pig.

favelas (fah-VEL-ahs) Slums in Brazilian cities.

feijoada (fay-ZHWAH-dah) Brazilian national dish, made of meat and black beans.

gaúcho (gah-OOH-shoo) Cowboy of southern Brazil.

guaraná (gwah-rah-NAH) Red rain-forest fruit, shaped like a grape, with a large seed inside; used to make a popular Brazilian soda.

mandioca (muhn-jee-AW-kah) Root vegetable that can be made into flour.

pampas (PUMP-ahs) South American prairies.

vestibular (ves-chee-boo-LAR) College entrance exam.

Proud to Be Brazilian

Edson Arantes do Nascimento (1940–   )

Have you heard about Brazil's shoeless soccer champ? Edson Arantes do Nascimento grew up near the city of São Paulo. Like many poor children, he learned to play soccer in the streets. Edson often had to play barefoot. When he finally joined an official team at the age of fifteen, he did not even own a pair of soccer shoes. The team bought him his first pair. Edson was such a good player that within two years he had joined Brazil's championship team. He led them to three World Cup victories. After eighteen years, Edson came to New York City, where he made soccer popular in the United States. He is the best-known soccer player in the world. He is called Pelé.

Princess Isabel (1846–1921)

One of Brazil's most beloved figures is a princess. Isabel was born more than one hundred fifty years ago in Rio de Janeiro. As a young girl, she often ruled the country when her father, Emperor Pedro II, was traveling. Isabel hated slavery. She was very upset that it was legal in Brazil. In 1888, while her father was away, she worked hard to pass "The Golden Law," which finally ended slavery. For this she won the love of her people and the nickname, *Redentora* (The Redeemer). After Brazil became a republic, Isabel moved with her husband to France, but her true home remained Brazil. Today people visit her memorial near Rio de Janeiro to remember Brazil's greatest princess.

Heitor Villa-Lobos (1887–1959)

Brazil's greatest composer owed his fame to a little train. Heitor Villa-Lobos was born in 1887 in a small city in the heart of Brazil. When he was twelve years old, his father died and young Heitor had to help support his family. He worked as a street musician, entertaining people for coins. He traveled from town to town on little rickety trains playing Brazilian folk songs. When Heitor grew up to be a composer, he never forgot the music or the trains. One of his most famous compositions tells the tale of a little train chugging across the hilly Brazilian countryside. It is called "Trenzinho do Caipira," which means little country train.

Find Out More

Books

Carnaval by George Ancona. Harcourt, California, 1999.

Festive Foods & Celebrations: Brazilian Foods & Culture by Jennifer Ferro. Rourke Press, Florida, 1999.

A Ticket to Brazil by Elizabeth Weitzman. Carolrhoda Books Inc., Minnesota, 1998.

The Way People Live: Life in the Amazon Rain Forest by Stuart A. Kallen. Lucent Books, California, 1999.

Web Sites

www.yahooligans.com/around_the_world/countries/Brazil
Links to just about everything, including maps and photos of Brazil, information on native peoples, and *Monica's Gang*.

www.sonia-portuguese.com
Learn to speak Portuguese like a Brazilian.

Video

Families of Brazil, from the Families of the World collection, Master Communication, 1999. VHS. 30 min.

Index

Page numbers for illustrations are in **boldface.**

About the Author

Bob Reiser, award-winning author and professional storyteller, has been telling tales and writing them down since his boyhood in Brooklyn, New York. His books with Pete Seeger, *Carry It On* and *Everybody Says Freedom*, are read across the country. His children's book, *David's Got His Drum*, co-written with Panama Francis, was published by Marshall Cavendish in 2002. He lives in Tarrytown, New York, with his wife Sandy, his son William, and his daughter Robin.